How to Be an Aztec Warrior

Written by
Fiona Macdonald

Illustrated by
Dave Antram
Mark Bergin

NATIONAL GEOGRAPHIC

Washington, D.C.

© The Salariya Book Company Ltd MMIV
Please visit the Salariya Book Company at **www.salariya.com**

First paperback printing 2008
First published in North America in 2005 by
NATIONAL GEOGRAPHIC SOCIETY
1145 17th Street N.W.
Washington, D.C. 20036-4688

Paperback ISBN: 978-1-4263-0168-1

Library of Congress Cataloging-in-Publication Data available on request.

Printed in China

Series created and designed by David Salariya
Penny Clarke, Editor

For the National Geographic Society
Bea Jackson, Art Director
Priyanka Lamichhane, Assistant Editor

Dr. Tim Laughton, Fact Consultant
Lecturer in pre-Columbian culture at the University of Essex

Photographic credits
t=top b=bottom c=center l=left r=right

Ancient Art and Architecture Collection: 25b
The Art Archive / Bodleian Library Oxford / The Bodleian Library: 18
The Art Archive / Mexican National Library / Mireille Vautier: 8
The Art Archive / Museo del Templo Mayor Mexico / Dagli Orti: 21
The Art Archive / Museo Etnografico Pigorini Rome / Dagli Orti: 13
The Art Archive / Museum für Völkerkunde Vienna / Dagli Orti: 12

The Art Archive / National Anthropological Museum Mexico / Dagli Orti:
11, 15, 23, 25t
The Art Archive / National Archives Mexico / Mireille Vautier: 17, 29
Every effort has been made to trace copyright holders. The Salariya Book
Company apologizes for any unintentional omissions and would be pleased,
in such cases, to add an acknowledgment in future editions.

One of the world's largest nonprofit scientific and educational organizations, the National Geographic Society was founded in 1888
"for the increase and diffusion of geographic knowledge." Fulfilling this mission, the Society educates and inspires millions every day
through its magazines, books, television programs, videos, maps and atlases, research grants, the National Geographic Bee, teacher
workshops, and innovative classroom materials. The Society is supported through membership dues, charitable gifts, and income from
the sale of its educational products. This support is vital to National Geographic's mission to increase global understanding and promote
conservation of our planet through exploration, research, and education.

For more information, please call 1-800-NGS LINE (647-5463) or write to the following address:
National Geographic Society
1145 17th Street N.W.
Washington, D.C. 20036-4688 U.S.A.
Visit the Society's Web site at **www.nationalgeographic.com**

Warriors Needed

How would you like to join the team that defends your people and your homeland?

The Aztec are looking for strong young warriors who are eager to seek adventure, win fame and praise for their bravery, and please the Aztec gods.

Your main duties will include:

- defending your city against invaders

- conquering new territory

- controlling conquered peoples and collecting tribute from them

- taking captives to sacrifice to the gods

(An interest in the Aztec Empire would be a great advantage.)

How to sign up? Hurry to the main square of your city when you hear the beat of the big war drum.

Contents

What You Should Know

Be prepared for a journey back in time—to the years between A.D. 1300 and 1500. That's when the Aztec were most powerful. From their capital city, Tenochtitlán (now known as Mexico City), they ruled a large empire in Mesoamerica, home to many different peoples. You'll find it's a harsh environment, full of contrasts. There are mountains, active volcanoes, deserts, and tropical rain forests. It's hot and dusty during the day, but bitterly cold at night. There are spiders, snakes, eagles, and jaguars. You'll see maize fields on mountain slopes, wild cacao trees that produce the beans used to make chocolate, and lakeside "floating gardens," where Aztec farmers grow chilies and tomatoes.

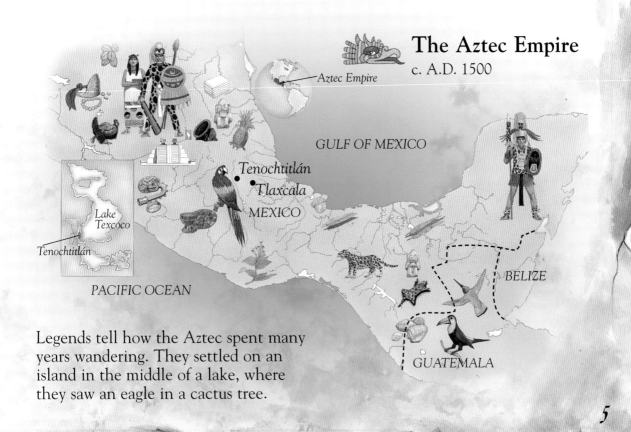

Aztec Empire

The Aztec Empire
c. A.D. 1500

GULF OF MEXICO

Tenochtitlán
Tlaxcala
MEXICO

Lake
Texcoco

Tenochtitlán

PACIFIC OCEAN

BELIZE

GUATEMALA

Legends tell how the Aztec spent many years wandering. They settled on an island in the middle of a lake, where they saw an eagle in a cactus tree.

Is Yours the Right Family?

Like all Aztec, you depend on your family for your place in society. Only nobles can be top military officers. Most soldiers come from ordinary families, with few possessions. You'll have grown up seeing your mother always busy—cooking, cleaning, weaving, and caring for your younger brothers and sisters. In his workshop or fields your father has taught you the skills you'll need to make a living.

▼ You live in a mud-brick house, with one room and a grass roof. A round granary, used to store maize, is in the courtyard outside.

Granary

Turkeys for food

Weaving

Foot plow for digging fields

Long cotton cloak

Fan

Noble privileges

◀ A boy from a noble family would have military duties, but he would live comfortably at home. He would have a big house, richly embroidered clothes, feather fans, gold jewelry, leather sandals, and lots of food. Slaves and servants would look after him and his family.

Tlatoani (emperor) Cihuacoatl (deputy ruler) Priest Government official Noble warrior Farmer

Thatch

Making tortillas

Mud-brick walls

Aztec society

▲ Aztec society is very unequal. The most powerful person is the Tlatoani (emperor). He lives with his family in a huge palace in Tenochtitlán. He is helped by a male deputy called Cihuacoatl (snake woman) and hundreds of government officials. The emperor also gets advice from the nobles who help lead the soldiers. Priests are very powerful. They study the stars, keep records, and perform sacrifices in the temples.

Cloak made of rough cactus fiber

Parents and children

▶ You may be a young adult, but you still live with your parents. Aztec parents are strict with their children, so they'll grow up respectful and obedient.

7

Are You Loyal to Your Clan?

Every Aztec belongs to a *calpulli*. This is a clan or large family group descended from the same ancestor. You'll have to obey calpulli leaders. They're in charge of law and order in your neighborhood, and organize such things as food and shelter in emergencies. Calpullis also run schools for boys and teach them to fight. If you want to be a warrior, your calpulli will help train you.

Calpullis

Calpullis control all the land in a neighborhood. If a farmer refuses to work his fields or a craftsman to tend his workshop, the calpulli can take it away and give it to someone else.

State taxes

To pay for government—and the empire's warriors—all Aztec farmers, craftworkers, and traders pay taxes to the emperor.

Don't try to cheat me or I'll complain to the government.

Stop worrying! We belong to the same clan.

Is poverty your fate?

◀ The Aztec believe that some people are fated by the gods to be criminals or to lead poor, unhappy lives. The goddess Coatlicue, shown in this drawing from an Aztec codex (book), was believed to bring slavery, poverty—and death.

Regular collections

Aztec give a share of their goods or crops to government officials, who collect them from calpullis every 20 days.

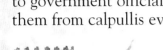

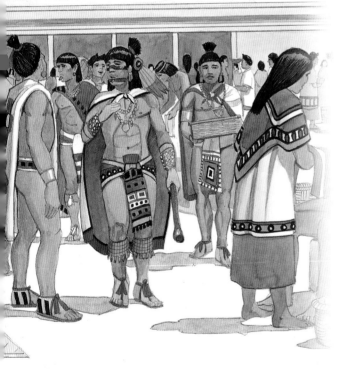

Law and order

Aztec laws are strict. They aim to frighten people into good behavior. And Aztec punishments are swift and severe. If you are found guilty of robbery, witchcraft, treason, or public drunkenness, you could be executed.

▲ Suspected criminals are brought before a judge.

▶ While waiting for the judge, suspects are locked in a wooden cage.

For a first offense, criminals may be pardoned or their house might be knocked down. For a second offense, there is no mercy. Guilty people are strangled (*above*) or clubbed to death (*right*).

◀ Aztec rulers also use bribes and rewards to help make people obey them. They offer gifts of gold to make friends with neighboring rulers. They give brightly colored cloaks to soldiers who take captives in battle.

9

Which School Did You Go To?

All Aztec boys go to school—but not all of them are taught to be warriors. When each boy is about 15 his parents have a choice. Should they send their son to a *calmecac* (temple school) run by priests or to a *tepochcalli* (house of young men) run by leaders of the local calpulli? Their decision will shape their son's future. Your parents decide on the house of young men.

▼ At a temple school, priests and scribes teach boys to read and write, as well as how to use three calendars based on holy tradition, the sun, and the planet Venus.

Picture books

▼ Aztec books (called "codices") are made of long strips of fig-bark paper, folded to make pages. The picture-writing is arranged zigzag across each page, from right to left then left to right, and from the top to the bottom.

Emperor

Sun god

Sketch the outlines in black, then add the colors with your brush.

▲ Scribes wrote using glyphs (picture symbols). Some glyphs showed items in miniature; others represented ideas. Each had its own sound. The glyphs could be combined, like letters, to spell long words.

Learning to be a warrior

If, like most Aztec boys, you went to a house of young men, you'll know nothing about reading or writing. Instead, you'll have been taught how to repair buildings, cut firewood, dig drainage ditches, and work on calpulli farms. You'll have spent your free time with friends, singing and dancing. There are restrictions on spending time with women during training. Most important of all, experienced warriors will have taught you to handle weapons and fight. They will also have instructed you to be brave and proud.

▶ Two pages of glyphs from the Codex Mendoza, written by Aztec scribes in the 16th century A.D. They show Aztec headdresses, clothing, jewelery, blankets, feather-trimmed shields, and warriors' uniforms.

Can You Handle Weapons?

Every man has to have his own weapons. Are yours ready? Do you have a bow and plenty of arrows, a stone-tipped spear, and a sling for hurling pebbles? Do you have a *macquauitl*—a strong wooden sword tipped with razor-sharp blades of obsidian (volcanic glass)? And don't forget your *atlatl* (spear-thrower) to launch plenty of javelins and poison-tipped darts.

▶ This feather shield is decorated with an *auitzotl*, a magic water creature. Priests say it kills people and sends their souls to the skies.

Extra protection

▼ As well as weapons, you'll need a shield. It is light but very strong. It will help fend off blows from enemy weapons.

Making a shield

Cut a wide strip of bark from a tree.

Soften it in lime and water.

Use a stone hammer to flatten it.

Your wife cleans some feathers.

Cut shield; strengthen with wood.

Glue the feathers onto the shield.

Uniforms and emblems

▲ How will you recognize your comrades in battle? Ordinary soldiers (*above left*) wear padded cotton armor soaked in saltwater to make it strong. Top warriors (*middle*) wear jaguar suits. Commanders (*right*) have huge flags or emblems strapped to their backs.

Stronger arms

▶ You'll use this wooden atlatl in battle or out hunting to help you throw darts and spears farther and faster. Hold the looped end in one hand and fix the spear or dart to the other. You'll find that the extra length the atlatl adds to your arm gives you extra throwing power.

Special footwear

▼ As an ordinary soldier you'll go barefoot. But if you're promoted to officer rank, you'll wear *cactli*—ankle-strap sandals of animal hide or braided cactus fiber. Top warriors wear sandals with elaborate lacing up to the knees.

13

Have You Had Your Hair Cut?

The Aztec have no official army. All men, even those who went to the temple school, are expected to do their duty and fight. Your first battle will be scary, but you will have a chance to show your fighting skills and prove you are a man. Until an Aztec takes his first prisoner, he cannot cut his hair.

The fate of prisoners

▼ Prisoners are sacrificed in many different ways. Sometimes, they are given weapons made of feathers, and forced to fight fully armed warriors. The blood they shed before they die is food for the gods.

Battle tactics

▲ Aztec battles are loud and extremely violent. At the start, warriors shout, blow bone whistles, and make fearsome booming noises on conch horns. Then archers and javelin-throwers rush forward to attack. Then come soldiers with spears and swords, advancing side by side in close formation.

Close combat

▼ When Aztec troops get close to their enemies they start fighting differently. They stop trying to kill the enemy soldiers or make them run away in terror. Instead, they do their best to capture them alive. Each Aztec swordsman fights hand-to-hand with a single enemy, hoping to overpower him. Special troops with ropes follow the Aztec swordsmen into battle. Their task is to tie up the captives and take them away.

A statue of the god Xochipilli

Important gods

▶ Xochipilli is a young man's god. He brings love, music, and dancing. He is honored by Aztec soldiers, along with Huitzilopochtli, a warrior god, and Mictlantecuhtli, god of the dead.

Will You Miss Home Cooking?

All Aztec know what it's like to go hungry. In years without rain you've seen maize shrivel in the fields and garden vegetables wilt and die. You've gone hunting for any food you can find—wild sage seeds, snakes, deer, cactus fruit, and lakeside algae. When you march off to battle, get ready to use those survival skills. You'll have to live off the land. It's a long way between towns with markets and warehouses of stored grain.

Feeding the family

▶ Aztec women spend hours every day cooking and serving food. It's hard work crushing dry maize kernels on a *metlatl*. Tortillas are the basic food. They are made from crushed maize and limewater. This mixture is kneaded and shaped into thin flat cakes before being baked on a griddle over a fire.

Other food

▼ Leaving home for war will not be easy. You'll miss your family. You love them, and you've gotten used to them taking care of you. Your mother feeds you, comforts you, and makes your clothes. Your little sisters help, too.

This is really good.

    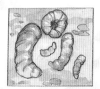

You can catch fish with traps, spears, or nets. You can net turtles and frogs, too.

Aztec think that lizards, fish eggs, and agave-cactus worms all taste delicious.

All-American

▶ The Aztec eat many plants and animals that at this time (around A.D. 1500) are found nowhere else on Earth.

Maize

Sweet potatoes

Tomatoes

Peppers

Turkey

Armadillo

Tapir

I hope you'll get enough to eat when you're away fighting.

Pottery griddle

Cooking methods

▼ Aztec have no iron or steel, so women use utensils of pottery or stone and an oven of sun-baked clay. They light a fire inside, rake out the ashes, then stew food in pots in the embers.

Clay oven

Pottery grater (rough inside)

Serving bowl

Warrior feast

◀ Women serve *pulque* (cactus beer) to guests at feasts. As a warrior, you'll share in many celebrations. The most important is "the great feast of the lords," held during the first seven days of the eighth month. The emperor provides food and drink, and soldiers sing and dance all night long.

17

Will You Be Able to Travel?

The Aztec Empire stretches from the Pacific Ocean to the Gulf of Mexico. You might live anywhere within this vast territory, with a military garrison controlling conquered land. You might march to defend the frontier or hurry to nearby Tlaxcala—where the Aztec are always at war. You'll see fine sights and meet new people. But traveling means walking, because the Aztec go almost everywhere on foot.

A fine capital city

▼ Tenochtitlán, capital of the Aztec Empire, is a magnificent city. More than half a million people live there. Huge temples surround its central square.

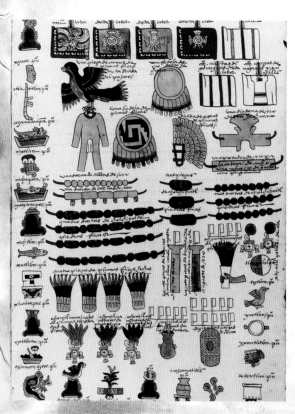

Riches for the emperor

◄ This page from Codex Mendoza shows why the Aztec Empire is so rich. It lists all the valuable tribute (forced gifts) that the emperor demands (and gets) from conquered territory—and from cities that wish to stay free of Aztec control. They send huge quantities of valuable produce to the Aztec capital. The emperor keeps some and sells the rest.

Roads and communications

▶ Roads link conquered cities throughout the Aztec Empire but there are no horses or wheeled transport. Urgent messages are carried in forked sticks by fast runners. Porters carry heavy loads.

Messengers, merchants, spies

The Aztec won their empire by fighting, and the emperor still uses the threat of war to conquer more land. First he sends messengers to ask the rulers of rich cities to submit to Aztec rule. If they do not agree he orders his warriors to attack. Emperors also send *pochteca* (merchants) to cities they want to conquer. The merchants act as spies, observing, remembering, and reporting all they have seen.

To expand the empire even more, past Aztec emperors made a Triple Alliance with two other powerful Mexican cities —Texcoco and Tlacopan.

Buying and selling

▼ Tlatelolco is a great market city, now part of Tenochtitlán. You reach it by canoe or a causeway. Tribute goods, craftwork, and food are sold there. Aztec have no coins, so they trade by barter (exchange) or use cacao beans or quills filled with gold dust.

Tribute goods

Cloak

Warrior's uniform

Feather shield

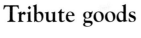

Basket of chilies

◀ These glyphs copied from a codex show some of the tribute goods sent to the Aztec emperor.

Can You Please the Gods?

Aztec believe the world is ruled by nature-gods who control the weather, the seasons, and time itself. The gods have destroyed and re-created the world four times already. This is the fifth, final, creation. If the gods destroy the world again it will be gone forever. So you must please them with festivals and sacrifices.

Measuring time

▼ The Sun Stone shows the four world ages that were created and destroyed by the gods. The face of the sun stares out from the center of the stone. Aztec honor more than 60 gods; all are different views of one supreme power.

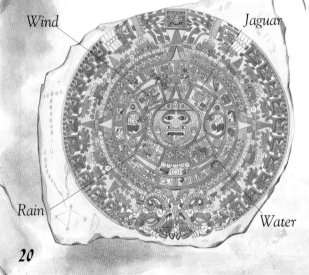

Wind

Jaguar

Rain

Water

New Fire ceremony

▲ The Aztec use two different calendars: the holy calendar for priests and scribes and the farmers' calendar for everyone else. Every 52 years both end at the same time. Aztec worry that the world will end then, too. They put out all fires and wait fearfully in the dark. When the stars appear, they sacrifice a man and light a new fire in his chest.

Temple fire

▶ Sticks from the burning sacrifice are used to light a new fire in the temple. Then the new fire is taken on lighted sticks to all homes in Aztec lands.

Human sacrifices

◀ This stone container shaped like an eagle held hearts from human sacrifices.

Feeding the gods

Aztec people see how the earth-gods provide food plants and the sky-gods send life-giving rain. They know that without these gifts they would die. They believe they must feed the gods in return, to show their thanks. So they give them human flesh and blood.

A prisoner to sacrifice

▶ If you capture prisoners in battle, they will be taken to temples for sacrifice by the priests. Their hearts will be cut out—and you will get some of their flesh to eat as a holy meal.

Are There Many Dangers?

You've seen enemy soldiers suffer horrible injuries. So you must expect your own life as a warrior might be full of pain from battle wounds. You may also suffer from fevers, ulcers, boils, and intestinal worms. All are part of daily life. Few Aztec live much longer than 40 years.

A doctor's remedies

▼ A *ticitl* (Aztec doctor) offers many different treatments. In battle, he'll bandage your wounds. Back home, he'll try herbal medicine, steam baths, or magic spells.

> I will try to cure you with powerful magic.

How to stay well

▶ You hope the gods will protect you. But you fear they might send disease if you offend them or break their religious rules.

Faith healing

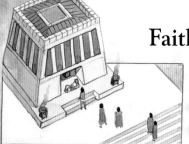

Go to a temple and let priests sprinkle you with holy water.

Make offerings of food to the gods, or kneel and say prayers.

Healing herbs

▼ Ticitls use more than 1200 medicinal plants, including some that are quite poisonous. If you die after treatment, Aztec say it is the will of the gods.

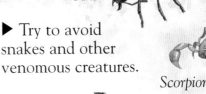
Ant

Scorpion

▶ Try to avoid snakes and other venomous creatures.

Spider

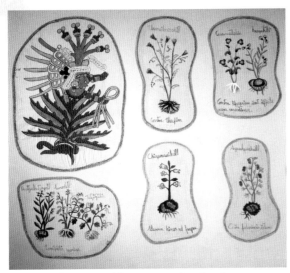

A page from a 16th-century book of herbal medicine

Magic and mystery

▼ Aztec believe that enemies can send magic weapons to harm them and that evil spirits and wandering ghosts can kill. Doctors may give you mind-altering drugs made from plants. They claim this will let your brain make contact with the spirit world so you can find out what is making you ill.

Tobacco

Peyote cactus

Psilocybin mushrooms

Morning glory

Steam bath

▼ Ticitls use steam baths to cure such illnesses as aching joints and colds. Patients sit in a mud-brick room filled with steam from the wood-burning furnace next door. They get very hot and sweat a lot; they hope this will cure them by driving out the illness.

What Rank Will You Be?

When an Aztec boy is born, the midwife buries his umbilical cord with tiny arrows and a shield and declares that his destiny is to fight. How well will you serve as a warrior? If you capture or kill four enemies, you can become an officer. You'll wear a feather headdress and take part in councils of war. After this you could be promoted to commander. But unless you are nobly born, you'll never be an eagle or jaguar knight.

Jaguar knights

▶ Jaguar knights are one of the two highest-ranking warriors. They wear jaguar skins and dedicate themselves to Tezcatlipoca, a warrior god. To the Aztec, jaguars are symbols of the underworld— and of silent strength and cunning.

Other careers for boys

▲ Strong and clever but no good at fighting? Become a government official.

▲ Prefer to be a priest? You may still fight. Some priests are also warriors.

▶ Stone portrait of an eagle warrior. He wears a feather-trimmed wooden helmet shaped like an eagle's head.

Eagle knights

◀ Eagle knights are the other top-ranking warriors. They train at a special college close to the great temple in the center of Tenochtitlán. They learn to be brave and withstand pain by making sacrifices of their own blood. In battle their duty is to risk their lives by leading the fighting. Their eagle uniform represents the sun shining brightly at dawn—a sign of new life, hope, and strength.

A deadly knife

▼ Sharp stone knives are used for killing captives as sacrifices. The handle of this knife shows the carved figure of a crouching eagle knight.

Could You Land the Top Job?

The first Aztec emperor gained power by defeating his opponents in battle. But now even the best warriors are unlikely to rule. For more than 100 years, all emperors have come from the same royal family. When an old emperor dies, military commanders, retired high-ranking soldiers, nobles, priests, and calpulli leaders all meet to choose one of his sons or grandsons to be the new ruler. Unless you've got royal blood, there's not much chance you'll get the top job.

▼ The emperor is head of the council of nobles and officials that runs the Aztec government. It's his duty to lead discussions of new plans.

▼ After an emperor is chosen, he makes sacrifices to the gods, then puts on splendid robes and goes out to meet the people.

Cermonial fan

The "four great ones"

In wartime the emperor is helped by noble officers known as "the four great ones." It is their duty to command divisions of the military and organize weapons and supplies. Usually they are members of the royal family, but if you are a truly exceptional soldier, the emperor might make you a "great one."

▼ Emperors travel in litters (portable couches) carried by nobles. As a sign of respect, his feet must not touch the ground in front of his people.

Headdress

Royal clothing

▲ Emperors wear special clothes to show their rank. Only they wear the *xicolli* (decorated vest). When they serve as priests, in rituals representing gods, they wear magnificent headdresses of quetzal feathers and gold.

An emperor's duties

The Aztec emperor has many duties. The most important are to direct the government and lead his people in war. He must also ensure that all citizens have enough food and water, build roads, protect temples, and conquer new lands. He leads discussions with neighboring rulers, controls trade and farming, and upholds the law. He takes part in religious rituals, praying and making offerings on behalf of all Aztec.

Aztec rulers

▶ The first Aztec ruler, Acamapichtli, reigned from about 1376–95 (*top left*); the last, Cuauhtemoc, c.1520–25 (*bottom right*). Glyphs depict the emperors and the arrival of Spanish soldiers.

Acamapichtli (1376-1395)

Huitzilihuitl (1396-1417)

Chimalpopoca (1417-1426)

Itzcoatl (1427-1440)

Moctezuma (1440-1469)

Axayacatl (1469-1481)

Tizoc (1481-1486)

Ahuitzotl (1486-1502)

Moctezuma II (1502-1520)

Hernan Cortés

Cuitlahuac (1520)

Cuauhtemoc (1520-1525)

Long-term Prospects

The Aztec believe that the gods have already decided the future. So what lies ahead for you? Will you die a glorious death in battle? Will you be captured, and possibly sacrificed, by the Aztec's enemies? Or perhaps you'll live long enough to fight against Spanish invaders. They will arrive in Mexico very soon and be welcomed by the emperor. But within two years they will defeat the Aztec warriors and destroy their empire.

▼ The Spanish invaders will have guns—unknown in Aztec lands.

One kind of afterlife

▼ If you're killed in peacetime, you'll travel to the underworld to the realm of Mictlantecuhtli, god of the dead. It's a long, painful journey that takes four years. When you arrive, you enter a state of nothingness and cease to exist.

A warrior's fate

If you die fighting bravely or as a sacrifice, you'll face a much happier afterlife. You'll spend your days in the sky with other dead warriors, singing and fighting mock battles as a "companion of the sun." After four years you'll be reborn as a hummingbird or a butterfly.

Outgunned by the Spanish

▼ Aztec warriors with their traditional weapons will be powerless against Spanish guns. They will ask Huitzilopochtli, their national god, for protection, but nothing can help them.

The end of the empire

▲ In 1519 Spanish soldiers, led by Hernan Cortés, will arrive in Mexico seeking gold. The Aztec will welcome them, believing they represent an ancient priest-king, Quetzalcoatl. But Cortés and his troops will defeat the Aztec, kill the emperor, and take control of Aztec lands. In 1535, they will make Mexico a colony of Spain, and Spanish settlers will arrive to live and rule there.

An Aztec's burial

▶ This codex picture shows a young man's body wrapped as a mummy-bundle and ready for burial. Beside him is food (beans and maize dumplings) for his journey to the underworld.

Your Interview

Answer these questions to test your knowledge, then look at page 32 to find out if you have what it takes to get the job.

Q1 What do ordinary Aztec soldiers wear on their feet?
A boots
B sandals
C nothing at all

Q2 What are glyphs?
A monsters summoned by witches
B picture symbols used in writing
C wild animals hunted for food

Q3 How do Aztec travel?
A by horse
B by tapir
C by foot

Q4 How does the emperor reward brave soldiers?
A by giving them colored cloaks
B by giving them land
C by giving them money

Q5 What are Aztec swords made of?
A iron
B gold
C wood and obsidian

Q6 Who is snake woman?
A the deputy emperor
B a witch
C a faith healer

Q7 What are warriors killed in battle reborn as?
A gods or goddesses
B hummingbirds or butterflies
C eagles or jaguars

Q8 Who may have to fight with feather swords?
A children
B magic birds
C prisoners being sacrificed

Q9 The holy calendar and the farmers' calendar both end after how many years?
A 12
B 52
C 100

Q10 What is the punishment for the second offense of a crime such as robbery?
A death
B a fine
C a warning

Glossary

Agave. Cactus with long, pointed, fleshy leaves.

Ancestor. Relative who died long ago.

Atlatl. Wooden spear-throwing device. It acted as an extension of the arm, so spears could be thrown with greater force.

Barter. Exchanging goods for others of equal value.

Cactli. Sandals of animal hide or braided cactus fiber.

Calpulli. Family or neighborhood group that owned land, provided education, and kept law and order.

Causeway. A raised road across water or marshland.

Conch shell. Large, horn-shaped shell of a marine animal called a conch.

Emblems. Designs or symbols that carry a message and are easy to recognize.

Glyph. Picture symbol. Glyphs were used in Aztec writing.

Granary. Building for storing grain.

Javelin. Small, light spear.

Limewater. A solution of calcium hydroxide in water.

Litter. Portable couch.

Maize. Corn.

Mesoamerica. Middle part of the American continent, from central Mexico in the north to Nicaragua in the south.

Metalatl. Curved stone for grinding grain.

Midwife. A person who is trained to assist women in childbirth.

Mummy-bundle. Dead body arranged in a sitting position and wrapped in layers of cloth before being buried.

Obsidian. Black glassy stone, produced when volcanoes erupt.

Pochteca. Aztec traveling merchants.

Quetzal. Rain forest bird with beautiful green feathers.

Quill. A feather's hollow, central shaft.

Sacrifice. Killing people or animals as a gift for the gods.

Tenochtitlán. The capital of the Aztec Empire; now called Mexico City.

Ticitl. Aztec doctor.

Tribute. Forced payment made by conquered peoples, or by those wishing to stay free of Aztec control.

Umbilical cord. Tube carrying blood from a mother to her unborn baby.

Xicolli. Decorated vest worn only by the emperor.

Index

Further Reading

Baquedano, Elizabeth. *Aztec, Inca, and Maya* (Eyewitness). DK Publishing Inc., 2000.
Steele, Philip. *The Aztec News.* Candlewick Press, 2000.

Have You Got the Job?

Count up your correct answers (*below right*) and find out if you got the job as an Aztec warrior.

Your score:

8 Congratulations! It's your destiny.
7 Nearly ready. Keep on training with your calpulli.
5–6 Promising. We'll keep you in mind if warriors are needed.

3–4 Not so good. Perhaps you should be a scribe or a priest, instead.
Fewer than 3 Perhaps you're destined to be poor.

Q1 (C) page 13
Q2 (B) page 11
Q3 (C) pages 18–19
Q4 (A) page 9
Q5 (C) page 12
Q6 (A) page 7
Q7 (B) page 28
Q8 (C) page 14
Q9 (B) page 20
Q10 (A) page 9